Gaia Servadio was born in 1938. She studied graphic art at St Martin's School of Art and typography at Camberwell School of Art before becoming a journalist and writer. Her first novel, *Tanto gentile e tanto onesta*, was published in Italian in 1967, with an English translation the following year. She has since written several other novels, two memoirs and a number of works of non-fiction, including biographies of Rossini, Visconti and Giuseppina Strepponi, Verdi's wife. Her subjects range from Siberia to the Mafia, archaeology, politics, history and music. She writes in both Italian and English, and many of her Italian works have been translated. During her long career she has also worked as a lecturer and broadcaster, and has made documentaries for the BBC.

Works by the same author in English

Fiction

Melinda (1968)

Non-fiction

A Siberian Encounter (1971)
Insider, Outsider (1978)
To a Different World: In the Land of the Mafia (1979)
Luchino Visconti (1983)
Mafiosi: A History of the Mafia (1989)
The Real Traviata (1995)
Motya: Unearthing a Lost Civilization (2000)
Rossini (2003)
Renaissance Women (2015)

Poetry

Tuscany & Umbria (Poetry of Place) (ed., 2011)

A WARTIME CHILDHOOD

GAIA SERVADIO

Translated from the Italian by
Maria Fairweather & Hero von Friesen

Published by The Cuckoo Press
for John Sandoe (Books) Ltd
10 Blacklands Terrace, London SW3 2SR

© Gaia Servadio
Adapated from *Un'infanzia diversa*, first published
in Italian by Rizzoli, Milan, 1988

English translation © Maria Fairweather
and Hero von Friesen 2020

The moral rights of the author and translators
have been asserted

A CIP catalogue reference for this book
is available from the British Library

ISBN 978 1 9998219 2 0

Designed by Fenella Willis

Printed and bound in the UK by CPI Group (UK) Ltd
Croydon, CR0 4YY

A WARTIME CHILDHOOD

April is the cruellest month, breeding
Lilacs out of the dead land, mixing
Memory and desire, stirring
Dull roots with spring rain.

The Waste Land
T.S. ELIOT

I

All of a sudden the big wooden box had become the centre of attention. It brooded imperiously on the corner table where, until recently, it had mostly been ignored. But now, since the fall of Mussolini, we listened to the radio all the time. Even though I was not yet five years old, I realised the importance of those voices that reached us through the hissing, peevish static. 'Hush, children! It's the news!'

Benito Mussolini was a name that I had heard since before I can remember. It was just a sound; it meant nothing to me. Photographs and portraits of Mussolini were everywhere, in offices, in people's homes and on the streets. His declarations, rendered in great block capitals, covered whole walls of houses in Padua and the surrounding countryside. They said unfathomable things about sheep and lions, Italy, bayonets, and more bayonets.

This name was often on the lips of the handful of people who made up my little world. I did not understand that the '*duce*' and Mussolini were even one and the same. It took the squawking radio to do that.

Roosting on the table above my head, the brown box emitted shrill whistles that hurt my ears; its loud cracklings interrupted the intense stream of talk that poured from it and took our parents' attention away from us. I could not follow much of what it said. I did at least grasp that nobody understood what was going on – that is to say, none of the people I knew: my parents, our nanny Isabella (whom we called Tata) and my sister Pucci. Mussolini had been arrested. But the war? What was this war, of which I had seen no sign in Padua but which everyone talked about? Some people thought that the war was wonderful – the big box, for instance, extolled it. But my father said it was a crime, and he argued with those few friends who came to play bridge. My father said the fascists were buffoons.

The fascists were the Italians – many of them, indeed almost all of them. Papà, rather flushed, would wrangle about bridge and politics at the top of his voice, calling everyone idiots. I would hear his passionate outbursts from the bedroom where Pucci and I slept.

II

The summer of 1943 was a hot one and, as usual, we spent August at the seaside. The factory where Papà worked never closed, so he would drive out to see us on Sundays in his car, a black Balilla. He was the young director of the SAICA factory, where they made tar, asphalt and chemical things with a smell of disinfectant that I loved. The factory belonged to Vittorio Cini, the 'doge' of fascist Venice.

Papà was really the managing director, except he wasn't – that is, not officially. Jews, according to the race laws, could not hold important jobs. The Italian racial laws were very severe but, as often happens with our laws, seldom observed; I do not think our family was much affected by them. Papà's salary was good, though less than he would have received had he been the official director, and our flat in the via del Corso was airy, with high ceilings and a fine balcony overlooking the river.

We had a maid as well as a nanny, despite the fact that Jews were not allowed to employ servants. We had a telephone in the house, although that too was forbidden by law. We even went away for our holidays. Pucci and I wore matching outfits with white socks and long skirts that reached below our knees.

Ladies used to invite Mamma to tea, and she would put on a little hat and gloves. We children went to a kindergarten run by nuns rather than the public primary school, because we were not allowed there. Neither could we join the Figlie della Lupa or the Piccole Italiane, so we could never wear those black uniforms I saw in the streets and in the park. I was very annoyed by that.

A bit late, and with some difficulty, Pucci and I had been baptised by the parish priest at the Church of the Eremitani (behind the back of the Bishop of Padua, who had refused us the sacrament). In 1943 we therefore counted as Catholics; but we were children of a mixed marriage, my sister and I. My mother was a Catholic, of a rather haphazard kind admittedly, but she was considered Aryan and that was what mattered. She was an anglophile. At eighteen she had spent a whole year in England, after which she had worked for the British Council in Rome as a librarian. She and my father had known each other since their school days. My father's family was Sephardic and came from Ancona, in the Marche, where they had been since the fifteenth century. They left the town for Rome after the bombardments of the First World War and the earthquake of 1930. And it was in Rome that my parents met.

Contrary to the stereotype of the avaricious and miserly Jew, my paternal grandfather, Nonno Cavour, spent freely and lived a very comfortable life with his five children and his wife Gemma, who came from a strict Jewish family in Turin. It was a large and happy family. The eldest, Lucia, was followed by four boys. These children were the light of his life, he used to say, and he gave them all names derived from '*lux*': Lucia, Luciano, Lucio, Luxardo (my father) and Luchino. He held secular and patriotic views; his friends used to tease him that he would call a sixth son Lucifer, a name that my grandfather in fact rather liked – 'the bearer of light'. Fortunately, perhaps, no sixth son was born.

Papà had just begun his studies at the university of Rome, aged nineteen, when his father died. He entered the science faculty at a period when modern chemistry and physics were still relatively new subjects; his university teaching assistants were none other than Pontecorvo, Fermi and Majorana. Though his future was secure as a chemist, it was never his vocation, for his natural bent was towards history and academia. From Rome he moved to Turin where he finished his studies; his first job took him to France, after which he returned to Rome. There he was appointed, very young, director of the factory in Padua.

So it was that Papà and Mamma, who had been married for a couple of years by then, left Rome with the greatest reluctance in 1938. Mamma was expecting her second child. After Pucci, their firstborn, they hoped for a little boy. Instead, to their great disappointment and to my father's dismay, I was a girl – born, moreover, in Padua, a city in which we had no roots at all.

The furniture in our flat in via del Corso was very high. Everything was enormous, Mamma and Papà too. And they were beautiful, at least to me. Papà was tall and he had elongated eyes; his hair was straight, combed back off his forehead as people did in those days. My mother's eyes were blue, almost violet, and she had wavy black hair. I wondered sometimes if my mother and father were actually beautiful, or if I just thought so because they were my parents and all children see their parents as beautiful. Of the grown-ups I knew, especially my parents, I remember only the faces, and especially the eyes. Even as a small child I had a very clear idea of aesthetics, which were important to me, and I divided everything into beautiful and ugly.

Pucci and I had friends with whom we played in the park near our house. Accompanied by Tata and always beautifully dressed, we used to go to a square in front of the Scrovegni chapel where there was an open patch of ground covered with dusty gravel. While Tata sat on a bench near the gate and chatted with a black-moustached policeman called Ugo, we played war with the other children, hiding our weapons – sticks – behind the hedges.

Isabella, our Tata, had black eyes and rippling hair. After a long series of nannies, she seemed destined to last in via del Corso. She wore a blue uniform with a white collar and gloves, and despite her southern accent I thought her very elegant. When she gave me a bath and washed my hair, she would tell me stories of sirens lacerated with knives, and naughty children mangled by spectacular acts of retribution from the heavens above.

Pucci used to tease me a lot. She had all the luck in the world, my big sister – most importantly she was the firstborn, with all the privileges which that entailed. During our afternoon nap, for example, when the sunlight filtered in long slivers through the shutters and I lay watching the tiny white particles of dust that danced about in the air as time seemed to stand still, Pucci would be reading illustrated books full of fascinating stories. She could read, so she wasn't bored. I didn't know how to read yet and, being 'the little one', I was supposed to sleep. That was the rule decreed by Mamma, Pucci and Tata. But at night, those same minute specks that had floated so delightfully in the sunlight became horrible demons, hollow-eyed and clawed, and I couldn't go to sleep.

On Sunday mornings, before lunch, Papà would take us out to buy pastries. This was a ritual, a pilgrimage. The pastry shop was also in via del Corso but beyond the park, near the Pedrocchi café. It was brilliant with mirrors that reflected swirling pastries with pointed tips, *cannoli* filled with ricotta and candied fruit, pyramids of glazed pine cones, caramel-coated seashells. When we got to the head of the queue, we would stand on tiptoe to see the wonders displayed in the glass cases. There were buttery pastries dusted with icing sugar, creamy pinnacles with cherries at the very top, and everywhere the heady smell of caramel that made us long to plunge head first into those beautifully arranged displays. Italy had been subject to trade sanctions since 1935, so coffee, chocolate and vanilla could only be obtained in ersatz form. But as I had never known the real things and had no idea of the true taste of coffee and chocolate, I did not suffer at all: for me those pastries were the *ne plus ultra*, the prize of the week. They made Sunday a holiday and made up for the boredom of the inevitable *passegiata* or the occasional mass at the Eremitani.

Sometimes we would make a trip out into the country. Carrying us on the bar of his bicycle or walking beside us, Papà would declaim poems by Leopardi and Petrarch, and even parts of the Divine Comedy, waving his arms in his grandiloquence. We understood absolutely nothing and would look at each other in desperation. But we did not dare rebel, and my mother paid no attention as she walked along, lost in her own thoughts.

So that summer, as usual, we spent the month of August by the sea, in Bellaria, a small town on the Adriatic. It was one of the few places where Jews were allowed to spend their holidays. I remember the avenues with oleanders in flower, pink and white, and the boarding house where we stayed, surrounded by a shady garden full of tall, dark trees.

Every morning we would go to the beach with Mamma and Tata, but after splashing about for a few minutes in the warm shallows we were always startled by the cry, 'Children! Out!' This draconian order was provoked by the outbreak of tiny wrinkles at the ends of our fingers, a sign of grave danger to our health: so said Mamma, and Tata echoed her. Only on Sundays, when Papà came, would a joyous anarchy break out. Papà let us wallow in the sea with our fingers all creased, and then played with us in the sand. He would dig huge holes and build a mountain that seemed gigantic. Then the ritual magic would begin. He would make a tunnel at the base of the mountain while we ran about looking for scraps of paper, straw and dry twigs. He would push these into the tunnel and set light to them, so that a triumphant plume of smoke would rise from a hole at the top, and sometimes even sparks. This attracted the attention and envy of the children under the neighbouring umbrellas: 'A volcano! A volcano!'

We returned from Bellaria to Padua but the weather remained very hot. The big brown box took centre stage once again when the Armistice of Cassibile, between the Kingdom of Italy and the Allies, was announced on the 8th September. I had no idea what an armistice was, nor was I interested; but my parents were extremely pre-occupied by it and talked of little else. Day by day, the vast German army stationed in Italy, our former ally, was becoming an enemy – that much could be understood.

A few days after the announcement, we all went north to Recoaro, close to the Dolomites, where we had rented a house to escape the heat of Padua and its many mosquitoes. Papà's mother, Nonna Gemma, and her mother, old Nonna Nina, had come to visit us in Padua and they came with us. I was terribly bored.

Towards the end of September, Papà came to collect us in a small truck that belonged to the factory. On the road he had passed German troops putting barbed wire on the hedges and burying mines in the ground in anticipation of the Allied invasion.

For us children, however, the ride back from Recoaro was great fun. The two grannies sat in the cabin beside Papà, who was driving, and we rode in the open back of the truck, where we had a fine view of the hills and countryside, of the vineyards spilling with grapes. Every now and then Papà would stop the truck, jump down and dash into a vineyard, to return with great bunches of grapes, black and white, golden and green. Our arrival back in Padua, on the other hand, was bitter. The Germans had arrived and there was a curfew. This was our first taste of that war we had heard so much about from the big wooden box, and we saw that it was a bad, ugly thing. On the bridge we saw scenes of violence – the very same bridge we crossed every day on our walks. The Nazis were roughing up civilians; their menacing uniforms and swastikas frightened us. It was then that I heard for the first time a word I would never forget: '*Schnell! Schnell!*' For them, everything had to be done quickly: you had to walk fast, even die fast.

After our return, Nonna Gemma and Nonna Nina remained for a while in Padua, to spend some time in the city and rest before travelling back to Turin, where they lived. Gemma was always somewhat severe, with an elegant, upright way of sitting. She wore dark dresses, often black, with lace collars that she fastened at the neck with an antique brooch. Nonna Nina, conversely, was very bent, and she spoke very little. She would sit and listen as her daughter played the piano; often she would simply gaze out of the

window. Nonna Gemma painted rather melan-
choly landscapes in the nineteenth-century style.
She had brought a stack of sheet music with her,
and would choose a piece and play it while I
watched. Those marks on the paper were just as
incomprehensible to me as the ones in her
Hebrew prayer books – mysterious and arcane.

III

One night after dinner, when we were already
in bed, Tata's friend Ugo, the policeman, came to
the door. He was out of breath because he had
come to the via del Corso secretly and in haste;
he wouldn't even sit down. Ugo said that the
Gestapo had gone to the police station and
demanded the list of all the Jews living in Padua.
Our names were on the list. At police headquar-
ters there was talk, he said, of camps where the
Jews were sent, and where they were massacred.
Trains went off to northern Europe and nobody
came back. Ugo gave a lot of details and said we
must escape right away – disappear as soon as
possible – immediately. It was a matter of life
and death. Papà and Mamma decided to leave at

once, keeping it secret even from us as far as possible. In just over twenty-four hours my father obtained false papers as our names were neither very Aryan nor very Catholic. Mamma put the silver in a safe place – or so she thought. The furniture went into the barn of a farmer friend; other things, household goods and family treasures, we buried in the country. Papà's Balilla was hidden under a haystack. In frantic haste they packed suitcases – just a few suitcases.

But our grandmothers were reluctant. Papà wanted Nonna Gemma and Nonna Nina to come along with us: we would all take a train for the south. The Allies had already landed in Sicily and soon they would capture the whole Italian peninsula. That was what the radio said, especially the clandestine voice which found its way through the howls and crackles to give us the real news – the 'voice of London', the BBC.

If we couldn't get through the front line, Papà said, we would stop in Rome, which, as an open city, would not be bombed. My mother's family were there and they would certainly help us and give us refuge. And there was also the Vatican in Rome, a neutral state.

But Nonna Gemma's home was in Turin; she had her piano there, her things. Nonna Nina was too old and tired to make such a strenuous journey, she said. Anyway, the fascists had promised amnesty to elderly Jews. So one morning Nonna Gemma and Nonna Nina came with us and our luggage to the station in Padua. They had their own suitcases, and when we departed for the south they would return to Turin. 'We are two old women, they'll leave us in peace,' they said.

Just a month later the fascists, minions of the Republic of Salò (the German puppet regime set up in 1943 by Mussolini after his rescue in the Gran Sasso raid), came knocking at their door: my grandmothers had been denounced to the Turin police by anonymous informers and were brought in. But the fascists in fact left them in peace, saying that they were old women and that there was a law that protected them, that they should not be afraid. They were allowed home. My grandmothers were also told, however, that they should move, disappear… But what could they do, old and rickety as Nonna Nina was? Where could they go? And how? Some time later the Gestapo arrived and took them away. Someone wanted their flat – that was almost always the reason why Jews were reported.

And so the two old ladies who had waved goodbye to us with fluttering handkerchiefs, as in an old film – and whom we had watched as they grew smaller and smaller in the distance, finally disappearing in a blur of tracks, platforms, lights and trains – the two old ladies were sent to the transit camp at Fossoli, and from there, in one of those death trains crammed with wretched people standing packed together without water or air, they were taken to Auschwitz.

Even after hearing Ugo's terrifying words, who could ever have grasped, or even imagined, such horrors?

It was around the end of September 1943 that we parted at the railway station in Padua. Our little family was excited – we children happy – because this unexpected journey would prolong the summer holiday. A new adventure was opening before us.

We travelled some three hundred kilometres and then came to a halt in Falconara, north of Ancona, because the trains could go no further. The railway tracks had been bombed; the lines of communication were, of course, the first targets.

IV

Falconara is quite near Ancona, a little over ten kilometres away. Papà and Mamma found us a flat on the ground floor of a house facing the sea. I remember it was a rectangular building whose design made no concession to aesthetics. But at the back of it there was a garden with pine trees and there, to our joy, was a swing. Looking along the shore of the Adriatic, we could see Ancona curving out to sea to the south-east, its ancient roofs rising up the slope of Monte Cardeto to its crown, the elegant Romanesque cathedral of San Ciriaco.

Papà had been born in Ancona and knew the dialect and region well. He bought a bicycle, which we often took into the hills on our excursions to try to buy food from the peasants. He would put me on the handlebars and off we would go, me perching happily with my hands on his shoulders. When we stopped at a farmhouse, sweet-smelling loaves would be brought out of cupboards. I used to love looking for hens' nests in the straw and running down the rows in the vineyards.

One day an Allied plane appeared, flying very low in front of the windows of our house.

'*Venite presto!*' shouted Papà, waving his arms, and then again in English: 'Come soon!'

A man on the road, passing the house on a bicycle, yelled to him: 'Can't you see? It's the enemy! It's an English plane!'

Papà pretended to have made a mistake. He called back, 'Oh, I thought it was German!' and closed the shutters.

It was not long before the bombings reached Falconara itself. One day a whole wall of our house fell down, part of the stairs caved in from the shockwave and the windowpanes shattered into terrifying shards. 'Children! Children!' screamed Mamma, searching for us desperately through the house and the garden.

The Germans ordered all civilians to evacuate the coastal area as they feared an Allied landing. Falconara had, in any case, become too dangerous for us because of the repeated air raids on the railway that ran through the town.

The problem was where to go, where to live while we waited for the Germans to lose the war. We were a family of lepers: anyone who took us in would be in danger. Papà was known in that region and there were people who would denounce Jews to the Germans in exchange for goods or money, or for the houses they lived in.

18

Papà's first thought was to go to Maiolati, a tiny village in the hills of the Marche where his old wet nurse lived. She was a peasant woman who had breastfed him for the first nine months of his life, and he was extremely fond of her. When she wrote to him – dictating because she was illiterate – she always ended the letter with these words: 'I leave you with my pen but not with my heart'.

However, the old woman's house in Maiolati was not big enough to accommodate a second family, and the peasants there were too poor to be able to part with food for us. Papà decided that the risk of denunciation in that sort of situation was too great, so he looked elsewhere.

He knew Gioconda Gallo, a woman who had a reputation for being hospitable to those in danger, and somehow he managed to reach her and speak to her. She offered him and his family refuge in Osimo, where the Gallo family had land and houses. But our Tata Isabella, who had managed to join us in Falconara, decided she would not follow us to Osimo. She wanted to go back to Padua and be with her Ugo, but promised she would never lose track of us and that we would meet again, perhaps in happier times. Isabella had serious problems in Padua:

Ugo's wife had discovered their relationship and made a horrific scene, with dire threats against both of them. I had no idea of all this, of course, but my sister suspected the truth.

Tata's place was taken by someone else: Nonno Cavour's sister, my father's aunt. She was named Italia, most patriotically. Zia Italia was a tiny, silent old lady with grey eyes, a childless widow who lived alone. Like us, she had to have false identity papers with names that did not sound Jewish, and she too needed to hide.

Before moving to Osimo, we had to go to the bank in Ancona to get money. I think my parents had decided to withdraw all we had left because of the runaway inflation. Besides, we needed a second bicycle. Papà decided to come with us to Ancona: all four of us 'women' were going – Mamma, Zia Italia and we two girls – and he didn't want to risk letting us go on our own. But Papà was a wanted man – indeed, all men were in danger then: they were considered deserters unless they belonged to Mussolini's Republican army. And the Nazis needed forced labour. By now everyone knew that wherever the Germans went, they brought death with them.

Mamma intuitively realised all this better than my father. She understood the danger, whereas

Papà sometimes treated the war as a sort of adventure. His life had completely altered from what it had been in Padua, when he ran the factory, came home to lunch every day and played bridge with his friends. Now he darted about the countryside on his bicycle and rather enjoyed making monkeys of the Germans, whom he considered an ugly, *petit bourgeois* tribe with no imagination. Though his career had been cut short by the racial laws, he was young and resourceful. But for my mother the sudden and drastic change had been more cruel. From one day to the next her name had become shameful; she had lost her home, her children were in constant danger, and her life, once so comfortable, was now one of hardship and poverty.

My mother foresaw the peril that threatened Papà were he to come with us to Ancona and a terrible row ensued: Papà refused to stay at home, and nothing she said could persuade him otherwise. As so often happened, it was in fact Pucci who decided the issue by bursting into tears. And so we women set off on our little expedition, leaving Papà to sulk in Falconara.

We took the train to Ancona and then walked for miles in a seemingly endless pilgrimage from one bank to another. I don't really know what happened or how much money Mamma managed to withdraw. As we walked, Zia Italia looked around at the streets she had lived in and knew so well, and saw them now ravaged by the bombings. In the old quarter, up on the hill, many streets were blocked by rubble; the city was nothing but a mass of ruins.

All four of us were walking along the main street of Ancona. Pucci and I were exhausted – how tired children get when they are bored! Zia Italia too, in her little black crocheted shawl, was trailing behind Mamma. Just then a line of trucks drove down the middle of the street and stopped, with the trucks about ten yards apart. Blackshirts and Gestapo climbed out and took up positions, moving slowly but precisely as if following a tried-and-tested script. Of course all this was noticed by the passers-by, who quickened their steps and tried to slip away into the side streets.

The Gestapo positioned themselves at the corners of the trucks, standing very straight with their machine guns aimed at the crowd. With a loudhailer, a Blackshirt thundered in Italian, 'Stay where you are! Nobody move! Silence! Anyone who moves will be shot!'

The street, so lively a few minutes earlier, was paralysed. People stood frozen, holding their breath, glued to the spot on the pavement where they found themselves at that instant.

I remember the scene well yet cannot say, looking back, how I reacted – certainly I was afraid, but I was always afraid in those days. Before we left Padua, my nocturnal fears had been the same as other children's. Now I had become afraid of other people, and of what they might do to harm me and my family. But events have a kind of inevitability for children – they do not recognise abnormality because they have no conception of what is normal.

My mother held us tightly. The Blackshirts and the Gestapo patrolled the street, grabbing all the men in the crowd and forcing them into the trucks. '*Schnell! Schnell!*'

They left the old men and little boys on the street. I stared at those men in the trucks as they looked about them with eyes wide: perhaps they would never again see those houses, those pavements. I knew this instinctively and understood that if Papà had come with us instead of staying angrily in Falconara, those black-clad men with the machine guns and sinister boots would have carried him off. Whereto, we did not know –

but surely to some cold and dreadful place, home to those evil men.

Pucci began to sob. My sister cried often; she was a nervous and watchful child. My mother approached one of the Blackshirts as he pointed a machine gun at the crowd. 'I have two little girls and an old lady with me,' she said. 'They're frightened, and I don't want to miss the last train.'

And so they let us go. I remember walking among those motionless people. With their pale, frightened faces, they looked like statues.

V

We left the next day – there was no time to lose. We set off on foot, as the bicycles were loaded with our baggage: packages, suitcases, a few blankets.

Zia Italia had gone up into the mountains a few hours before us, in a wagon pulled by a good mule. She had found refuge in a village near Iesi. I was sorry to leave Falconara, the sea, the garden and especially the swing. Before our departure, Pucci and I gave a sort of show on the swing, using scraps of material and improvised costumes, telling stories of heroes and princesses. We sold 'tickets' not only to our parents but also to some neighbours who had the patience to watch such a spectacle.

The road to Osimo was long and dusty and all uphill. It seemed to go on forever. By the roadside the hedges were grey with dust, and even the few small farmhouses were dust-coloured. Now and then, when one of us got too tired to walk, Papà would put us on the saddle of one of the bicycles and push us. At long last, after passing Osimo's railway station – which stood on flat ground nearly three kilometres from the town – we came to the white road that led straight up the hill to the massive ochre walls of Osimo itself. The Roman walls framed a panorama of bell towers and pinnacles that looked like a mediaeval fresco. The sky was lit up by a blazing sunset. We had arrived – at last we had arrived!

It was night by the time we entered the town. In the dark we found our way through the streets to Palazzo Gallo, which gave onto a rectangular piazza that seemed enormous to me. The façade of the *palazzo* seemed grand and elegant, as did the entrance hall with its scrolls and slightly rustic eighteenth-century stucco decorations. The porter's lodge was ready for us: we were to play the part of the new guardians of Palazzo Gallo.

That small ground-floor apartment contained two little rooms with two beds in each, leading off from a square, very empty room that Papà did his best to decorate, trying to transform it into a sitting room. The lavatory was truly tiny, and the kitchen consisted of a small stove in a corner of the so-called sitting room. We had so little to eat, however, that a kitchen more worthy of the name would have been useless.

The Gallos were friends of Papà. Their families had known each other for years, and they not only took us in but tried to help us in every way they could with furniture and blankets. Autumn was coming and Osimo was high in the hills; already it was beginning to get cold. Pucci's feet were growing as fast as the rest of her. Mine, at least for the moment, were sure of inheriting the shoes outgrown by my sister, but poor Pucci had no shoes of her own. Papà tried in vain, with scissors and nails, to make her old ones longer. He even went to the nearby town of Loreto where, despite all the halt and lame who were miraculously healed at the sacred shrine, he could not procure the much more simple miracle of a pair of shoes for his elder daughter.

Again we listened to the radio, the latest of a long line of brown wooden boxes, which had appeared on the little table that was the only furniture in the 'sitting room'. We heard the news, as usual preceded by the warning, 'Hush, children! Be quiet!' The familiar severe chords announced the 'voice of London', which spoke of armies and distant lands that I knew nothing of. Then it gave messages for the partisans, in code, such as 'the ewe is in the farmyard' or 'the calf is sleeping'. For months the 'voice of London' had been broadcasting news of German victories, but now we began to hear of defeats.

Listening to the 'voice of London' was forbidden, of course, but at the hour of the broadcast priests and friars and all sorts of people would come to our place to hear the news. They listened in silence, even when, as often happened, the words were drowned out by bursts of static. Afterwards there would be an explosion of comments, rising and falling waves of discussion hushed by cautious gestures: everywhere there were hostile ears that might hear and inform the Germans.

Pucci and I played in the piazza outside

Palazzo Gallo, or in the courtyard behind the building. There were no gardens or trees nearby – in fact, Osimo seemed to consist only of bricks. The streets were cobbled with smooth, shiny stones that hurt the soles of our feet, especially mine, which felt every bump. The houses, built close together, allowed little light into the narrow lanes. But it was wonderfully bright in the piazza in front of the Palazzo Gallo and in the main street leading from it to the old town hall and the cathedral. To me these all seemed very far away.

Every now and again Pucci and I were admitted to the first floor, the *piano nobile*, where the Marchesa Gallo lived with her daughters, two young women. The apartment was dark and intimidating, decorated with eighteenth-century portraits of ladies with puffy lips and voluminous silk dresses. When we climbed the stairs into the deepening shade of the first floor, we found the adults having tea in a large, crepuscular drawing room, very elegant with its stuccoes and frayed damasks. Pucci and I would curtsey, eat a biscuit or two – how we would have loved to fill our mouths and pockets with all those luscious confections! – and go back to the porter's lodge, while Papà and Mamma stayed upstairs playing bridge.

Life was far from normal but to make it seem more so, our parents decided that we should go to school. Pucci, always bright and diligent, would go back into the third year, while I was to enter the first. The school was near Palazzo Gallo. To get there you went behind the *palazzo*, through the labyrinth of dark little lanes, down a narrow street, and then, twisting down another dark alley, you came upon the school. In Osimo, everything was close by.

Early in the morning we would set out and trot to school through those cramped alleyways. In one I found the opening to a printer's work-shop, announced by the scent of ink and print-ed paper. I used to stop at the dark doorway, through which came the clatter of machinery and other interesting metallic sounds, squeezing myself just inside.

There, in two dustbins, I found lots of pieces of paper. Sometimes I would get my hands dirty with printer's ink – half dried and a bit sticky, sweet-smelling – as I rifled through the bins trying to find good bits for drawing. Everything was used frugally during the war, so I found only strips of pulpy paper, rectangular but very narrow, on which I had to draw long, long creatures. Once in a while I would even find white paper in the bin, but it was always in small scraps. I would fill my satchel and continue on my way to school.

I remember very little of that school in Osimo. I don't think I learned much there.

Pucci and I arrived all scrubbed and tidy on our first day, smiling timidly and hoping that the other children would like us. Quite suddenly someone asked me, 'What's your name?'

'Gaia Servadio,' I answered serenely.

Pucci moved closer to me and corrected what I had said in a confidential tone: 'My sister is so little she doesn't even know her own name. Her name is Gaia Prinzi.'

I felt humiliated. I'd been caught out. I had forgotten about my new names – 'Gaia Prinzi' was in the fact the most recent of several versions. Anyway, why should I have to remember any name that was not my own? Who had decreed that my name was 'not right'? That it was even dangerous? I felt as if I was carrying a strange contagious disease, a disease I could neither identify nor feel, but of which I was ashamed because it made me different. Clearly I was different from other children even though they, just like me, lived through the fear of those days, the terror of the bombs. But in what way I differed from them I did not know.

Small children accept things easily and adapt themselves. Nevertheless, I considered this difference of mine a personal defect – as if I had a hump on my back without being aware of it. I learned to be dismayed by the sound of my own name. Many years later, at the Ardigo primary school in Padua and then at the Liceo Romagnosi in Parma, I would wait apprehensively for the teacher to read the register aloud every morning. When she came to the fatal letter 'S' and that strange name that was mine, that defined me, I had to stand up and say 'present' to a chorus of jeers that came especially from the boys' side. Those jeers were not imaginary, but perhaps I magnified them in my timorous anticipation. I felt all this as a nightmarish shadow that menaced my family: perhaps I had to pay for sins of theirs, some crimes I did not know about.

VI

I have no idea how it came about but one day a tattered piece of paper arrived at Palazzo Gallo.

31

It brought a message, written in pencil, and it came from Fossoli, the transit camp near Carpi in the province of Modena from which the trains left for northern Europe. It was from Papà's mother, Nonna Gemma. She begged my father to send her paper and pencil and warm clothes, because they lacked everything. She said that she and old Nina were suffering from hunger and cold, they had nothing. She even asked for a comb.

By the time that missive arrived – necessarily by slow and tortuous routes – Nonna Gemma and her mother had probably already been gassed in the extermination camp at Auschwitz.

When she read the note, my mother realised at once that it meant the two poor women were dead; she sat down in a corner and wept. But to my father the implication was not so clear – how could it have been? Who could ever have conceived the idea of genocide, the suffocating trains, the humiliation and the massacre at the end of the journey?

Until a short time ago, whenever I happened to remember my grandmother and her mother, I would avert my mind and try to think of other things, as one might cross the street to avoid something unpleasant, such as the carcass of a dog. But then, later, I tried to imagine the wagons packed with other people just like them, victims who did not understand why they were in that situation and in those conditions, without water, without air, without food. I pictured them standing, tightly packed together, for days and nights, some dying of suffocation and privation, and then the arrival at the terminus from which every train returned empty. And the selection under the reflectors, and being forced to walk into the gas chambers, the death that was too slow and too conscious, and that chimney that smoked because, in the words of an SS man who worked in the crematoria, 'Human flesh burns well.'

Much later my father managed to find out what had happened to his mother and grandmother. At the end of the war Papà, like so many others, went to the station in Verona to wait for the trains returning from the Brenner Pass. He stood at the end of the platform amidst a crowd of people with strained, anxious faces. They waited for days, and every time a train came in they would throw themselves upon the living skeletons that emerged from the carriages. Many carried placards with photographs and the names of loved ones who had been deported.

And the emaciated, brutalised survivors were bombarded with questions: 'Have you seen… ?' 'Did you meet… ?' 'Do you know… ?' But those who returned from the terror did not want to linger on its memory. They pushed away the pleading hands, the faces, the questioning eyes, so desperately anxious to know and so reluctant to accept the truth. They wanted only to forget – everything, and at once.

Several months later, perhaps in 1946, my father ran into a young woman from Turin whom he had known as a girl; she was a survivor of Auschwitz. She said to him, 'I'll tell you because you insist, but don't ask me any more questions, don't ask me anything, and don't come looking for me again. Because I don't remember anything – I don't want to remember anything.' In the extermination camp she had been employed in the transportation of corpses to the furnaces of Birkenau. She told my father that his mother and grandmother had been lucky, for they were sent to the gas chambers at the first selection and died soon after their arrival.

EPILOGUE

Papà wrote a note for himself. He kept the page for the rest of his life.

I have it still: 'Our Gemma, transported late June 1944; 650 people from Fossoli to Auschwitz-Birkenau, Upper Silesia. Information from Anita Gembichi (?) The train travelled for about eight days. Approximate date of their martyrdom 2–4 July 1944.'

In 1944 Nonna Gemma and Nonna Nina were rounded up by the Nazis and the fascists of the Republic of Salò, overseen by the Ministry for the Purity of the Race, whose head was a former Jesuit called Preziosi, as ferocious as the harshest Nazi. Our grandmothers were taken to Fossoli, near Carpi, where they survived for a month in terrible conditions. In June they were transported to Auschwitz on a cattle train with no food or latrine.

A year or so after the end of the war, in mid-1946, Nonna Gemma's brother, Adolfo Vitale, went to Auschwitz.

Because of the racial laws, he had been dismissed from his high-ranking post in Cirenaica, the Italian colony in Libya, and went to Paris. When that city was occupied by the Nazis,

Adolfo fled to the south of France and later joined his niece Zia Lucia and her family in Tangier, where he worked for the US delegation. After the Liberation, he was sent to Rome with one of the first Allied convoys. There he witnessed the despair of so many who were looking for their lost relatives that he set up the CRDE, the Comitato di Ricerche Deportati Ebrei. Later, in Poland, he represented the new Italian government at the trial of the Auschwitz commander Rudolf Höss, who was convicted as a war criminal and sentenced to death. He brought my father a handful of ashes from the rubble of the crematoria, which my father kept in a drawer.

★

Papà wrote a beautiful epitaph for his mother's empty tomb in the Jewish cemetery in Ancona:

Non qui le spoglie mortali di
Gemma Vitale Servadio
Ma lontane, disperse confuse negli orrori
dei campi di Auschwitz.
A eterna accusa di tanta tragedia umana e famigliare
A ricordo di quella che incarnò

le più nobili doti di madre
Lucia Luciano Lucio Luxardo Luchino
Questa lapide pongono con pietosa devozione
e tenero affetto.
1878–1944

Not here the mortal remains of
Gemma Vitale Servadio
But far away, scattered in the horrors of the
camps of Auschwitz.
In eternal indictment of so much human
and familial tragedy
In memory of one who incarnated the most
noble gifts of motherhood
Lucia Luciano Lucio Luxardo Luchino
Place this stone with pious devotion
and tender love.
1878–1944

A few years ago, I went to Ancona with my
sister and we drove up to the cemetery as
evening fell. It was about to shut. We stopped at
the lodge and asked the old guardian to help us
with directions. I remembered that the Jewish
cemetery was at the very top of the hill, with a
view of the sea, and difficult to find. Leaning out
of a window, the guardian told me to come back

the next day.

'I will be gone, I'm taking a ferry to Greece.'

'All right, then. My grandson will take you,' he answered.

A small boy in shorts appeared from nowhere, with large eyes and a smile. He was spending his school holidays with his grandfather, in the cemetery.

'Aren't you frightened at night?' I asked, stupidly.

'My grandfather says that one should be frightened of the living, not of the dead.'

We stood a while amongst those tombs and then we left, our little guide leading the way and refusing my grateful tip.

A NOTE ON THE TEXT

These pages are culled from Gaia's memoir of her childhood, published in Italian by Rizzoli in 1988 as *Un'infanzia diversa*. She was happy when, in the early 1900s, her great friend Maria Fairweather decided to translate it into English. There is also a more recent version of that translation, considerably revised by Gaia in the early 2000s, with much additional material. The text of this Cuckoo Press publication draws on all three of these, using MF's translation as a starting point and then working from the Italian. Many passages are new translations in their entirety. The epilogue appears in neither the Italian original nor MF's translation. All footnotes have been elided but a few small additions have been made to the text for clarification.

HvF

★

John Sandoe's and The Cuckoo Press hope to publish the full text of Gaia's memoir in the future.

MARIA FAIRWEATHER (1943–2010) was of Greek and Armenian parentage; she was born and brought up in Tehran. A linguist, she was the author of two books, *Pilgrim Princess: A Life of Princess Zinaida Volkonsky* (1999) and *Madame de Staël* (2005). She married a British diplomat whose postings included a stint in Rome from 1992 to 1996. They had two daughters.

HERO VON FRIESEN is Scottish on her mother's side and German-Austrian-American on her father's. Her paternal grandparents emigrated from Germany in 1934, renouncing their German citizenship a few years later. She has a background in archaeology and languages, and has worked as a translator, editor and researcher for various publishers and cultural organisations. In 2012 she joined John Sandoe's, where she is better known as Arabella or Boojum...

★

John Sandoe's is very grateful to Sir Patrick Fairweather for his kind permission to use his late wife's work.